FISHING

Gary Newman
with thanks to Selena Masson

 Crabtree Publishing Company
www.crabtreebooks.com

Crabtree Publishing Company

www.crabtreebooks.com   1-800-387-7650

Copyright © **2009 CRABTREE PUBLISHING COMPANY**.

**Published
in Canada
Crabtree Publishing**
616 Welland Ave.
St. Catharines, ON
L2M 5V6

**Published in the
United States
Crabtree Publishing**
PMB16A
350 Fifth Ave., Suite 3308
New York, NY 10118

Content development by Shakespeare Squared
www.ShakespeareSquared.com
First published in Great Britain in 2008 by ticktock Media Ltd,
2 Orchard Business Centre, North Farm Road,
Tunbridge Wells, Kent, TN2 3XF
Copyright © ticktock Entertainment Ltd 2008

Author: Gary Newman
Project editor: Ruth Owen
Project designer: Sara Greasley
Photo research: Ruth Owen
Proofreaders: Robert Walker,
    Crystal Sikkens
Production coordinator:
    Katherine Kantor
Prepress technician:
    Katherine Kantor

With thanks to series
editors Honor Head and
Jean Coppendale,
www.theessentialfly.co.uk
and www.flyfishingusa.com.

Thank you to Lorraine
Petersen and the
members of nasen

Picture credits:
Alamy: Chad Ehlers: p. 22 (left); Simon Grosset: p. 22 (right);
    Stock Connection Distribution: p. 20–21, 23
J. L. Allworks: p. 13 (top), 13 (center); The Essential Fly: p. 19
Angling Times: p. 1, 4 (top)
Ian Chapman: p. 8 (center), 10
Corbis: Roy Morsch: cover; George Shelley: p. 18 (bottom)
Henry Gilbey: p. 2–3, 5, 14–15, 17 (top), 18 (top)
IGFA (International Game Fish Association): p. 31
Shutterstock: p. 6–7, 16
Steve Lockett: p. 26–27, 28, 29
SuperStock: age fotostock: p. 17 (bottom); BilderLounge: p. 24–25
ticktock Media Archive: p. 12, 13 (bottom)
Max Tremlett: p. 4 (bottom)
Roy Westwood: p. 7 (top), 8 (top), 8 (bottom), 9, 11

Library and Archives Canada Cataloguing in Publication

Newman, Gary, 1976-
    Fishing / Gary Newman.

(Crabtree contact)
Includes index.
ISBN 978-0-7787-3769-8 (bound).--ISBN 978-0-7787-3791-9 (pbk.)

1. Fishing--Juvenile literature. I. Title. II. Series.

SH445.N49 2008   j799.1   C2008-906085-7

Library of Congress Cataloging-in-Publication Data

Newman, Gary, 1976-
    Fishing / Gary Newman.
        p. cm. -- (Crabtree contact)
    Includes index.
    ISBN-13: 978-0-7787-3791-9 (pbk. : alk. paper)
    ISBN-10: 0-7787-3791-8 (pbk. : alk. paper)
    ISBN-13: 978-0-7787-3769-8 (reinforced library binding : alk. paper)
    ISBN-10: 0-7787-3769-1 (reinforced library binding : alk. paper)
    1. Fishing--Juvenile literature. I. Title. II. Series.

SH445.N49 2009
799.1--dc22
                                                                2008040145

CONTENTS

GONE FISHING

Fishing is more than just catching fish. It is the **anticipation** of the **bite**. It is enjoying the outdoors and the fresh air.

People who fish are called **anglers**. Anglers who fish in freshwater are called **freshwater anglers**. Freshwater anglers fish in lakes and rivers. They catch fish such as carp, pike, and catfish.

Carp

Flies

Fly fishing is catching fish using **lures** called **flies**. Fly fishing is done in rivers, streams, and other fast-moving fresh water.

Anglers who fish in salt water are called **saltwater anglers**. Saltwater anglers fish in seas and oceans. These anglers can fish from a beach, a dock, or rocks.

Saltwater anglers can also catch big game fish, such as marlin, shark, or tuna, from a boat.

Saltwater fishing for bass

FRESHWATER FISHING

There are two main ways of freshwater fishing —
using **floats** and using **sinkers**.

Big carp hide in
weeds at the
edges of the lake.

People use floats to
keep the **bait** near the
surface of the water.

Float

Predatory fish, such as
pike, zander, perch, and
catfish like shelter. They
hide in plants and reeds.

Tench and crucian
carp like to hide
under lily pads.

Many different baits can be used for freshwater fishing
- Worms and minnows
- Bread, cheese, and corn
- Specially made **boilies**

Boilies

People use sinkers to weigh down the bait. Sinkers pull the bait into deeper water.

Bream feed in flat, weed-free areas such as behind gravel bars.

Sinker

A DAY ON THE BANK

Today, I'm fishing for carp on a lake. I have seen some carp jumping at one end of the lake.

I **cast** to the area where I saw the fish.

My bait is inside a **PVA bag** of **feed pellets**.

The bag will dissolve and leave the pellets on the bottom of the lake. They will attract the carp to my bait.

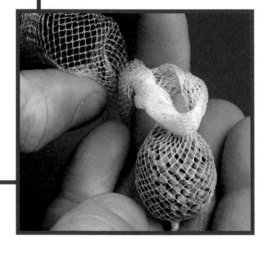

Bite alarm

The line runs through an **electronic bite alarm**. When a fish pulls the line, it sets off the alarm.

After a few hours, the alarm goes off. **It is a carp!**

The **clutch** on my reel is set properly. This allows the fish to take line. A carp can take 164 feet (50 meters) of line from the reel when it is first hooked.

9

CARING FOR THE CATCH

People who fish for sport put the fish back in the water after catching them. Other anglers can then enjoy catching them.

Always use a **landing net** to **land** the fish.

Keep the fish out of the water just long enough to unhook, weigh, and photograph the fish.

Landing net

It is important that fish go back into the water in the same condition as when you caught them.

Unhooking mat

Big fish should be laid on a padded **unhooking mat** while you unhook them.

If you do not want to release the fish right away, you can keep it in a **keepnet** for a short time.

Keepnet

A keepnet should be properly spread out. It should be put in deep water in the shade.

LURES

Lures are a great way to catch predatory fish such as pike, zander, and bass.

Lures are made from metal or plastic. Some are shaped and painted so that it looks like a real fish.

Plug lures *look the most real.*
They are ideal in clear water for wary fish.

You can use a special lure rod with your lures. A lure rod is designed to make the lure look like a real fish as it moves through the water.

Different lures attract different fish. Always carry a selection so you can try different ones.

Spoons reflect the light as they wobble through the water.

*Spinners spin around a fixed stem.
This movement attracts the fish.*

Lure bags are great for short fishing sessions. You can keep many lures ready to go at any time!

Lure bag

FLY FISHING

Fly fishing is one way to catch fish such as trout and salmon. Anglers use a long, **responsive** rod, a reel, and a line.

For bait, they use **imitation** flies. The flies look like the insects which are the fish's natural prey.

This Atlantic salmon was caught using a fly. The water was so clear that the angler was able to spot the fish and cast the fly directly to it.

FLY FISHING - CASTING

To perform a basic fly fishing cast, grip the rod as if you are shaking someone's hand. Pull as much line as you think you need off the reel. This line will sit in a pile at your feet.

Think of your casting arm as a clock's hour hand.

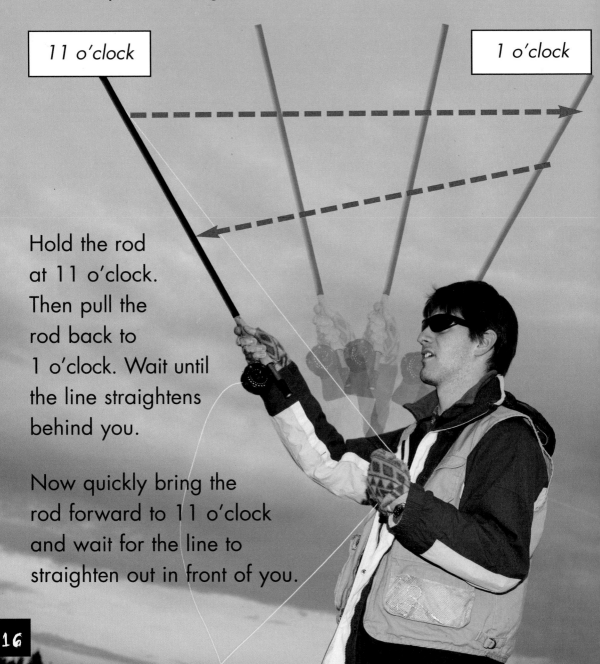

11 o'clock

1 o'clock

Hold the rod at 11 o'clock. Then pull the rod back to 1 o'clock. Wait until the line straightens behind you.

Now quickly bring the rod forward to 11 o'clock and wait for the line to straighten out in front of you.

Keep working the rod backward and forward. As you do, allow more and more line out through your fingers.

When your line is long enough to reach your target, let the fly drop onto the water.

FLIES AND GEAR

Flies look like the insects that the fish eat. They are made from fur, feathers, and thread tied onto a sharp hook.

Whipping tool

Vice

Tying flies is tricky work! But it is great to catch a fish with a fly you have tied yourself.

Fly fishing anglers wear vests with many pockets for storing gear such as fly boxes and sunglasses.

They also wear long, rubber boots or all-in-one boots and rubber pants. These are known as **waders**.

Vest

Waders

Net

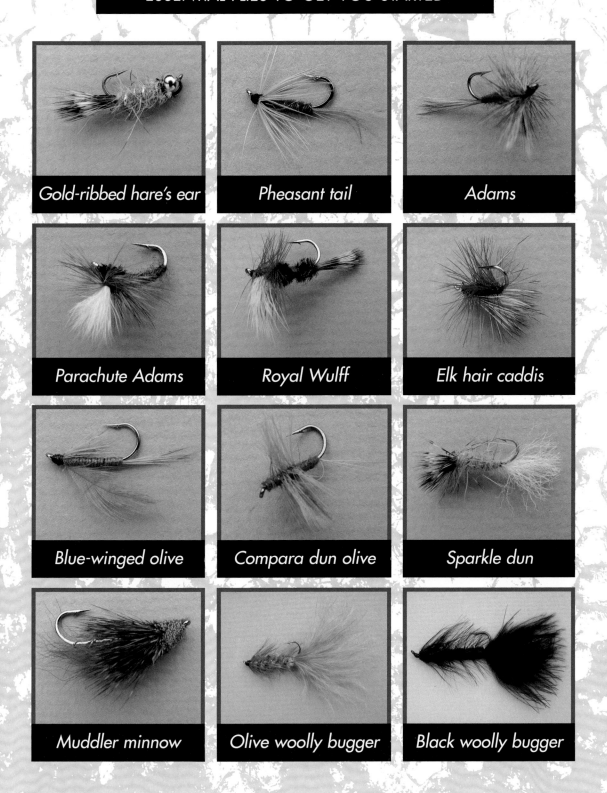

Gold-ribbed hare's ear	*Pheasant tail*	*Adams*
Parachute Adams	*Royal Wulff*	*Elk hair caddis*
Blue-winged olive	*Compara dun olive*	*Sparkle dun*
Muddler minnow	*Olive woolly bugger*	*Black woolly bugger*

The fly choice depends on which insects
the fish are eating at that time of year.

Blue marlin can swim more than 50 mph (80 km/h).

Some saltwater anglers like to fish for
big game fish such as marlin, tuna,
and shark. This type of saltwater fishing
is known as **big game fishing**.

Marlin are large, powerful fish.
This makes them difficult to catch.

The largest ever blue marlin caught
on a rod and reel weighed over
1,015 pounds (460 kilograms)!

CATCHING A MARLIN

Big game fishing is done from a boat. Anglers can **charter** a boat with an experienced crew.

Big game rod

Reel

Marlin lure

Marlin anglers use extra strong rods with thick lines.

They use lures that look like squid — the marlin's main food.

Anglers can also use natural bait, such as mackerel, combined with a lure. These are called "skirted baits."

Marlin can be found in warm oceans in places such as the Caribbean, South America, Africa, Australia, and New Zealand.

A string of **teasers** is pulled behind the boat. This is known as **trolling**. The main lure is on the end, so it is first to be hit by the marlin.

Charter boat

Main lure

"Catching a marlin must be every angler's dream. To be on a boat when a marlin **strikes** is an amazing experience. To hear the crack of the line when it leaves the **bait clip**. To see an enormous fish on its tail jumping out of the water.

It is a long, hard fight to get these fish to the boat. But it's the best feeling when you're holding the fish's **bill** and you release it to swim for another day."

Ali Boyd, big game angler

MATCH FISHING

The World Match Fishing Championships is the most important competition for many anglers because they represent their country.

The championship is held in a different country each year. Teams from all over the world enter. Each team has five anglers.

A lake or river is split into five sections. One angler from each country fishes each section.

It does not matter how many fish you catch or what size they are. Your total weight of fish at the end of the two days is what counts.

The angler who catches the most pounds of fish wins a gold medal. The winning team also gets gold.

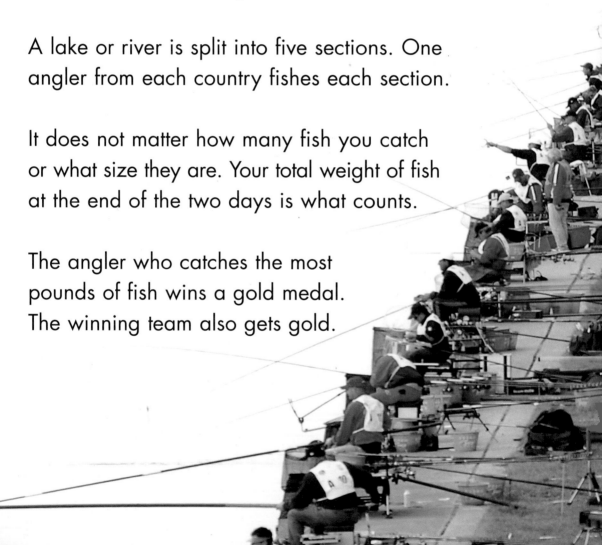

The 2007 championships in Hungary

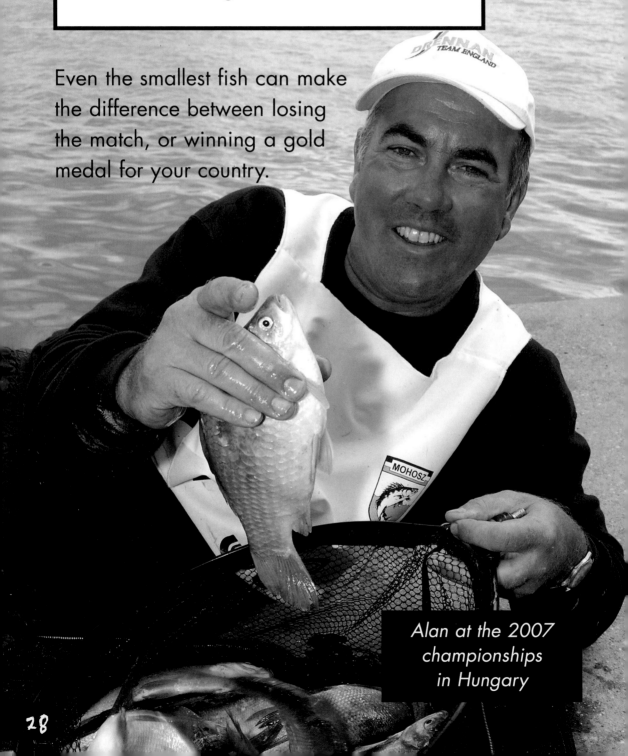

CHAMPION ANGLER

British angler Alan Scotthorne has won the individual gold medal five times.

Even the smallest fish can make the difference between losing the match, or winning a gold medal for your country.

Alan at the 2007 championships in Hungary

"I've been fishing since I was six. My dream was just to get into the England team.

The first time I won was in Italy. It was unbelievable! Italy had a strong team so it was great to beat them at home. We go as a team, so the team gold is the most important."

Alan Scotthorne

Winning a fifth gold medal in Hungary 2007

"The best feeling was winning individual and team gold in Croatia in 1998, and having two gold medals around my neck!"

Alan Scotthorne

NEED-TO-KNOW WORDS

angler A person who catches fish using a rod and line

anticipation Looking forward to something

bait Food used to tempt fish

bait clip A piece of equipment that holds the line in place. When a fish takes, it releases the line

bill A long, pointed, bony snout

bite When a fish takes the bait

boilie A specially made fishing bait. Boilies are balls of paste with different flavors. They can be bought from fishing tackle shops

cast Using a fishing rod to throw bait into the water

charter To hire a boat and its crew

clutch Part of a fishing reel. It allows line to be pulled off the spool by a fish. Without a clutch, your line would snap

electronic bite alarm An alarm that goes off when a fish has taken the bait

feed pellets Small ball-shaped pieces of food to attract fish

flies Fishing lures made to look like a fly

imitation Something that looks like, or pretends to be, something else

land To bring a fish to land

landing net A net with soft mesh for landing a fish

lure A man-made bait used to catch fish

predatory The word to describe an animal that hunts and eats other animals

PVA bag A type of plastic bag that dissolves in water. PVA bags are filled with food to attract fish

responsive Something that responds well. A responsive rod makes the actions you need quickly and accurately

strikes Another word for a fish taking the bait (see bite)

teaser A lure or piece of bait that is used to attract a fish, but which doesn't have a hook

trolling A method of fishing where one or more fishing lines are dragged behind a moving boat

CATCHING A RECORD

There are two types of records for anglers — national records and IGFA records.

see *http://www.igfa.org/*

- If you catch a record-breaking fish, you will need someone to witness your catch. Another angler is the best witness.
- Weigh the fish in front of your witness. Contact the record-keeping organization to let them know.
- Get your scales checked to make sure they are accurate. Fill out the claim form.

An IGFA record-breaking 15lb 12oz (6.9 kilogram) largemouth bass. It was caught by 11-year-old Mackenzie Ruth Hickox.

FISHING ONLINE

www.catchfishing.com/
Free printable booklet full of fishing tips for young anglers

www.ncfisheries.net/kids/
Information about saltwater fishing

www.takemefishing.org/fishing/overview
Useful information for young anglers

Publisher's note to educators and parents:
Our editors have carefully reviewed these websites to ensure that they are suitable for children. Many websites change frequently, however, and we cannot guarantee that a site's future contents will continue to meet our high standards of quality and educational value. Be advised that children should be closely supervised whenever they access the Internet.

INDEX

Printed in the U.S.A. - BG